Alfred's Kid's Drum Course 2 (Late

The Easiest Drum Method Ever!

Dave Black • Steve Houghton

MW00444562

Cover and interior illustrations by Jeff Shelly.

Alfred Publishing Co., Inc.
16320 Roscoe Blvd., Suite 100
P.O. Box 10003
Van Nuys, CA 91410-0003
alfred.com

Contents

Preface

After completing *Alfred's Kid's Drum Course*, Book 1, you should have a good foundation and understanding of certain basic rhythms, counting, drum rudiments, musical terms, form and notation, improvisation, coordination and ensemble playing. Book 2 continues the building process by establishing sound playing techniques and a better knowledge of the rudiments. Improved improvisational skills, drumset skills and the ability to play with an ensemble will be introduced in the process. As with the first book, body drumming has been woven throughout to help the player internalize the rhythms and understand the movement associated with each rhythm.

As with Book 1, a specific drum or instrument is not required. Remember, musical sounds can be produced with simple, inexpensive objects found around the home. Book 2 will continue our exploration of drumming and rhythms by taking a trip around the world, learning rhythms and musical styles from a wide variety of countries. Learn, have fun and enjoy the trip.

Acknowledgments

The authors wish to thank Karen Farnum Surmani, Kate Westin and Bruce Goldes for their invaluable assistance in the preparation of this book. A very special thanks to Rich Eames for his engineering, orchestrations, and multi-keyboard talents.

About the CD

The CD contains many of the exercises and all of the tunes included in this book, so you can listen and play along with them. The CD tracks also serve as a model to help strengthen time keeping, improve ensemble playing, clarify phrasing and expand your knowledge of musical styles.

Selecting Your Sound Source

A *sound source* is anything used to create musical sound. Traditional instruments, such as drums, are the most commonly used sound sources, but other objects can be used as sound sources as well. Non-traditional instruments include everyday objects that can be found at home or made in the classroom, as well as a variety of manufactured items designed with fun and creativity in mind.

Drums and accessory (extra) percussion instruments come in a variety of shapes, types and sizes. It's important to choose an instrument that's just the right size for you, and not one that's too big or too small. Holding your instrument should look and feel comfortable. When you are ready to purchase a drum or percussion accessory, it's a good idea to have your teacher or a music store specialist evaluate whether it is the right size for you.

For a partial list of traditional and non-traditional percussion instruments and sound sources, please refer to *Alfred's Kid's Drum Course*, Book 1, page 4.

General Practice Tips

1. Keep a regular practice schedule.

2. Count out loud and keep a steady beat.

3. Practice the rhythms and exercises slowly at first, then play them along with the CD.

4. Keep a practice diary.

5. Enjoy practicing. Playing drums is fun!

Basic Music Notation Review

Before starting this book, you need to know all of the following things that were taught in *Alfred's Kid's Drum Course*, Book 1. If there's anything you don't remember, go back to that book and review it. Once you are comfortable with all these things, you are ready to start with *Alfred's Kid's Drum Course*, Book 2.

Getting Ready to Play

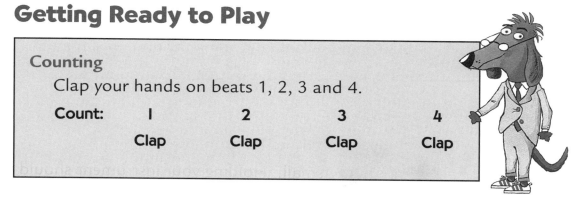

Counting

Clap your hands on beats 1, 2, 3 and 4.

Count:	1	2	3	4
	Clap	Clap	Clap	Clap

Reading Music Notation

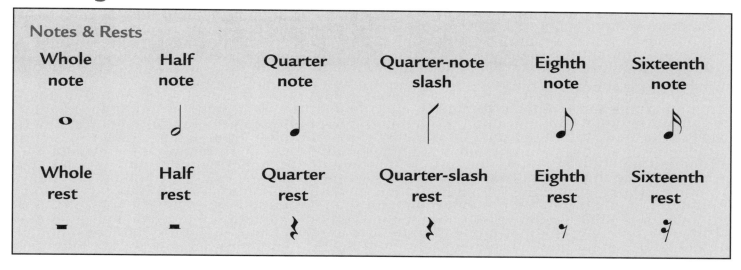

Notes & Rests

Whole note	Half note	Quarter note	Quarter-note slash	Eighth note	Sixteenth note
Whole rest	Half rest	Quarter rest	Quarter-slash rest	Eighth rest	Sixteenth rest

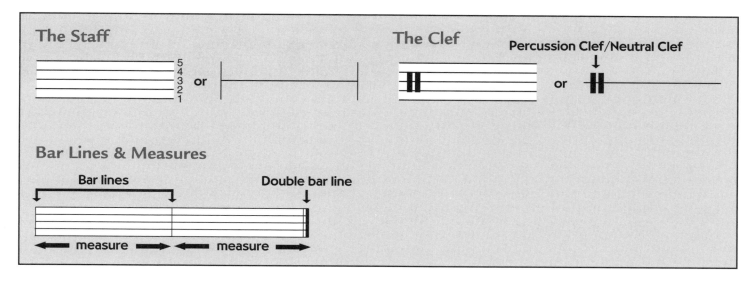

The Staff

The Clef

Percussion Clef/Neutral Clef

Bar Lines & Measures

Bar lines   Double bar line

measure   measure

Time Signatures

A $\frac{4}{4}$ *time signature* (called "four-four time") means there are four equal beats in every measure, and a quarter note (♩) gets one beat.

Time Signature

or

Count: 1 2 3 4

Repeat Sign

Double dots on the inside of a double barline mean to go back to the beginning and play again.

Basic Playing Techniques

Let's Review the Matched Grip

1. First, extend your right hand as if you were going to shake hands with someone.

2. Place the stick between your thumb and first finger at the fulcrum point (A).

3. Curve the other fingers around the stick (B).

4. Turn your hand over so your palm is facing towards the floor (C).

5. Repeat steps 1–4 with your left hand.

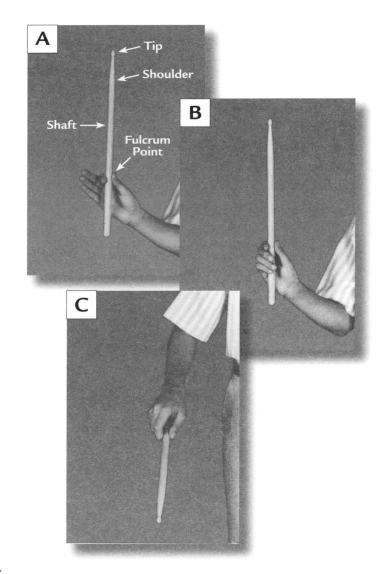

6

Three-Tempo Rock Track 1

Play three times: first time **Andante**, second time **Moderato**, third time **Allegro**.

R.H. (Sound Source 1)

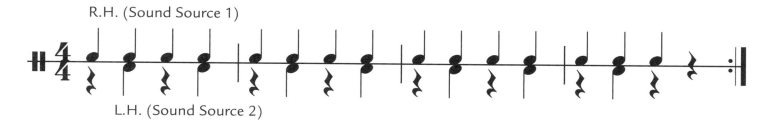

L.H. (Sound Source 2)

7

Review: Skip to My Lou

This is a good song to review because it includes many of the basic music notation concepts you learned in Book 1. Before Playing along with the CD, practice the part alone until you are comfortable with it. Start slowly and gradually increase the tempo. Repeat this song once.

Skip to My Lou

Track 2

Allegro (♩ = 126-132)

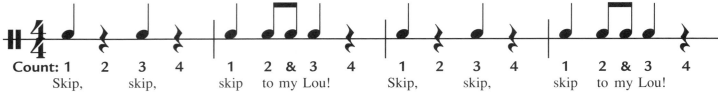

Count: 1   2   3   4   1   2 & 3   4   1   2   3   4   1   2 & 3   4
Skip,   skip,   skip to my Lou!   Skip,   skip,   skip to my Lou!

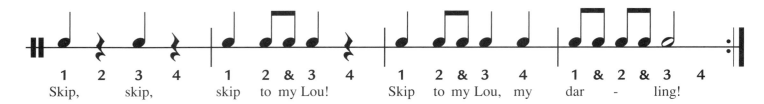

1   2   3   4   1   2 & 3   4   1   2 & 3   4   1 & 2 & 3   4
Skip,   skip,   skip to my Lou!   Skip to my Lou,   my   dar - ling!

Introducing Dynamics

Symbols that show how loud or soft to play are called dynamics. These symbols come from Italian words. Four of the most common dynamics are shown here.

p	***mf***	***f***	***ff***
piano	*mezzo-forte*	*forte*	*fortissimo*
("Pee-AH-noh")	("MED-zoh FOHR-tay")	("FOHR-tay")	(fohr-TEE-see-moh)
soft	**moderately loud**	**loud**	**very loud**

My First Dynamics Track 3

The following example uses all four dynamic levels. Be sure to look ahead and notice where the dynamics appear in the music. Before playing along with the CD, listen to the track first so you can hear the difference between each of the dynamic levels.

Allegro (♩ = 132)

R.H. (Sound Source 1)

L.H. (Sound Source 2)

The Tide Rises and Falls Track 4

The following example uses a crescendo and a decrescendo.
As the music gets louder, can you picture the waves rising?
As the music gets softer, can you picture the waves getting smaller?

Crescendo	*Decrescendo*
("kreh-SHEN-doh")	("deh-kreh-SHEN-doh")
gradually getting louder	**gradually getting softer**

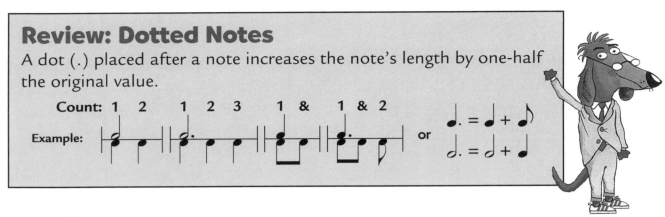

Review: Dotted Notes

A dot (.) placed after a note increases the note's length by one-half the original value.

Practice Warm-Up

Practice the following rhythm patterns until you are comfortable with them. Start slowly, and gradually increase the tempo. Be sure to count!

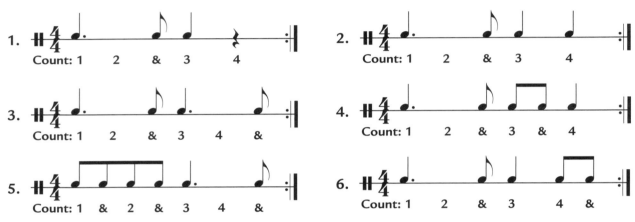

Dotted-Note Duet Track 5

A duet is a musical composition for two voices (singers) or instruments (players). Use two different sound sources for this duet. Before playing along with the CD, practice each part separately until you are comfortable with it. Start slowly, and gradually increase the tempo.

Sha Lee Hung Ba Track 6
(A Chinese Folk Song)

Use two different sound sources for this song. Before playing along with the CD, practice each part separately until you are comfortable with it. Start slowly, and gradually increase the tempo.

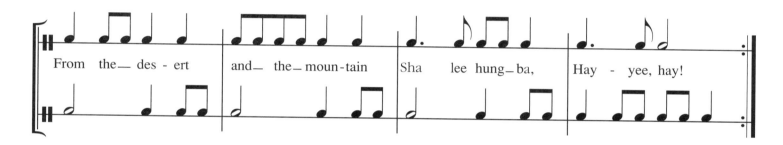

Review: Body Drumming

You can also use your body as a sound source to tap out the rhythms. Your body's "drumset" includes hand claps, foot stomps, finger snaps, leg pats, chest pats and head pats.

Go back and play track #6 again using two different sound sources (hands, feet, etc.). Both parts can be played by one person.

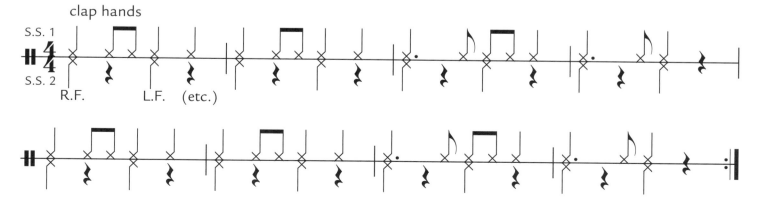

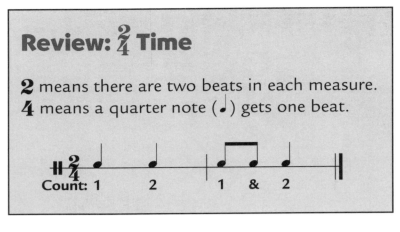

Review: $\frac{2}{4}$ Time

2 means there are two beats in each measure.
4 means a quarter note ($\quarternote$) gets one beat.

Count: 1   2   1 & 2

Grasshopper Track 7
(A Japanese Folk Song)

Use two different sound sources for this song. Before playing along with the CD, practice each part separately until you are comfortable with it. Start slowly and gradually increase the tempo.

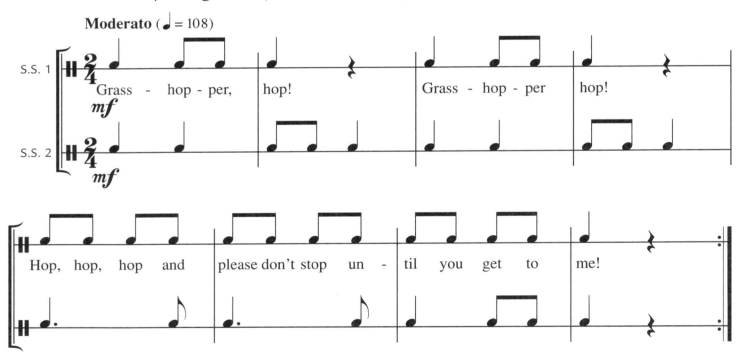

Moderato ($\quarternote$ = 108)

S.S. 1 — Grass - hop - per, hop! Grass - hop - per hop!

mf

S.S. 2

mf

Hop, hop, hop and please don't stop un - til you get to me!

Body Drumming

Use two different sound sources (hands, feet, etc.). Both parts can be played by one person.

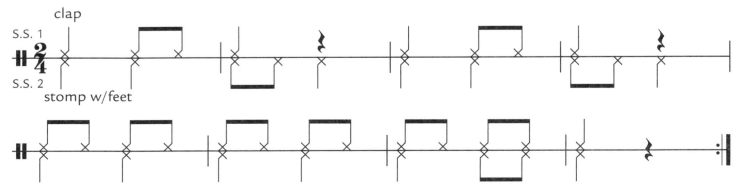

clap

S.S. 1

S.S. 2

stomp w/feet

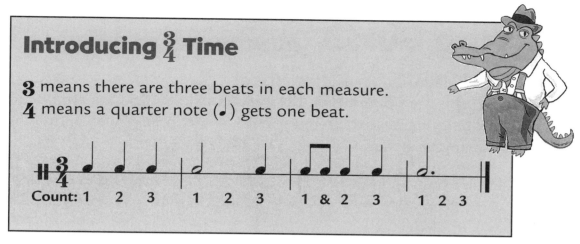

Introducing ¾ Time

3 means there are three beats in each measure.
4 means a quarter note (♩) gets one beat.

Count: 1 2 3 1 2 3 1 & 2 3 1 2 3

Three is for Me! Track 8

Use two different sound sources for this duet. Before playing along with the CD, practice each part separately until you are comfortable with it. Start slowly and gradually increase the tempo.

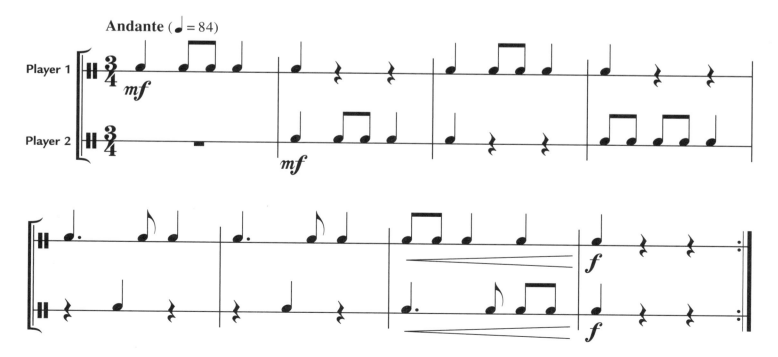

Andante (♩ = 84)

Player 1

Player 2

Paru-Parog Bukid (Meadow Butterfly)
(A Filipino Folk Song)

Before playing along with the CD, practice the part alone until you are comfortable with it. Start slowly and gradually increase the tempo. This song can be played with either a sound source, or leg pats with your hands.

Introducing Ties

A *tie* is a curved line that connects two notes. When two notes are tied, don't play the second note, but keep the first note playing until the second note is done. You are really adding two notes together.

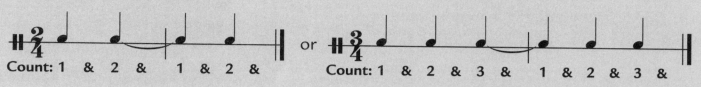

Practice Warm-up

Clap or play the following exercises. Make sure you count out loud.

All Tied Up Track 10

Use two different sound sources for this duet. Before playing along with the CD, practice each part separately until you are comfortable with it. Start slowly and gradually increase the tempo.

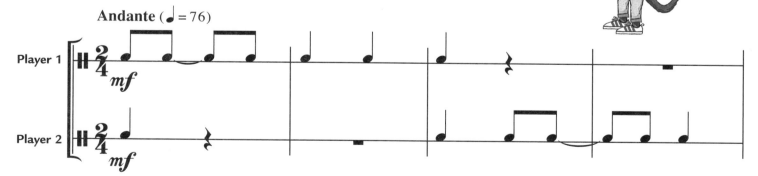

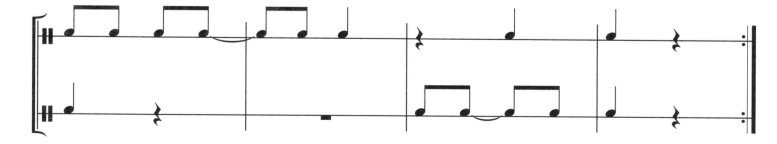

15

Chacarera Track 11
(An Argentinean Folk Song)

Before playing along with the CD, practice the part alone until you are comfortable with it. Start slowly and gradually increase the tempo. Play this song four times.

Allegro ($\bullet$ = 144)

guitar introduction—don't play

play four times

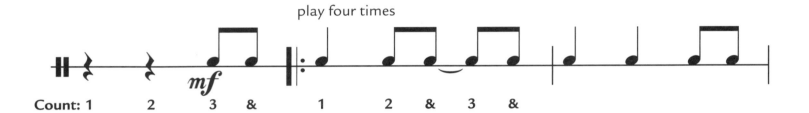

Count: 1   2   3   &   1   2   &   3   &

1   2   &   3   &   1   &   2   &   3   &

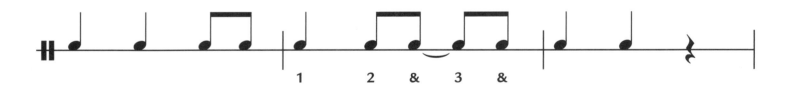

1   2   &   3   &

guitar—don't play

play

Count: 1   2   3   &   1

Review: Sixteenth Notes

Two or more sixteenth notes are joined together by a *double beam*.

Four sixteenth notes are played in the time of one quarter note.

Practice Warm-Up

Practice the following rhythm patterns until you are comfortable with them. Start slowly, and gradually increase the tempo. Be sure to count!

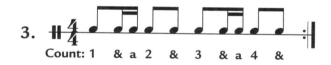

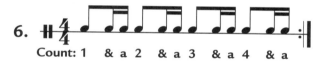

Sixteenth-Note Duet Track 12

Use two different sound sources for this duet. Before playing along with the CD, practice each part separately until you are comfortable with it. Start slowly and gradually increase the tempo.

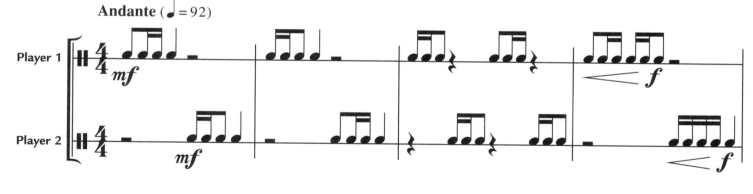

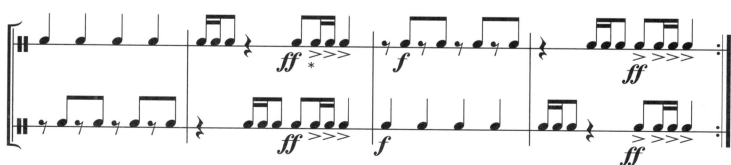

*> = Accent. Play the note a little louder.

Hi-Yah-Ho  Track 13
(A Chinese Folk Song)

Use two different sound sources for this duet. Before playing along with the CD, practice each part separately until you are comfortable with it. Start slowly and gradually increase the tempo.

18

Review: Trio

A trio is a musical composition for three voices (singers) or instruments (players).

La Bamba Track 14
(A Mexican Folk Song)

Use three different sound sources for this song. Before playing along with the CD, practice each part separately until you are comfortable with it. Start slowly and increase the tempo.

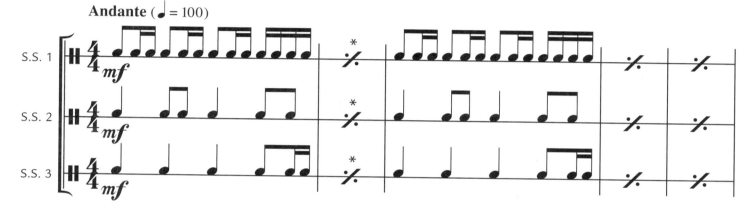

Body Drumming Use three different sound sources (hands, feet, etc.).
Play 4½ times.

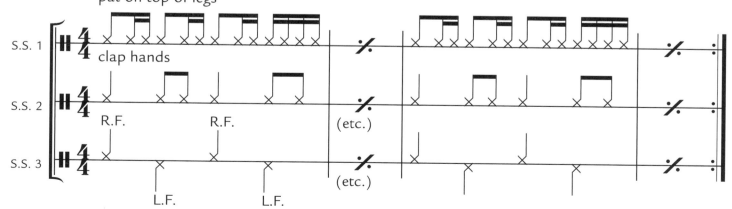

* This sign ⅟ tells you to repeat the previous measure.

19

Don Simon
Track 15
(A Puerto Rican Folk Song)

Use two different sound sources for this song. Before playing along with the CD, practice each part separately until you are comfortable with it. Start slowly and increase the tempo.

Cajueiro Pequenino  Track 16
(A Brazilian Folk Song)

Use three different sound sources for this song. Before playing along with the CD, practice each part separately until you are comfortable with it. Start slowly and increase the tempo. Wait for the four-measure guitar introduction before playing.

Play eight times.

Andante ($\quad$ = 96)

*Play first seven times only.

Body Drumming

Use three different sound sources (hands, feet, legs, etc.). Play eight times.

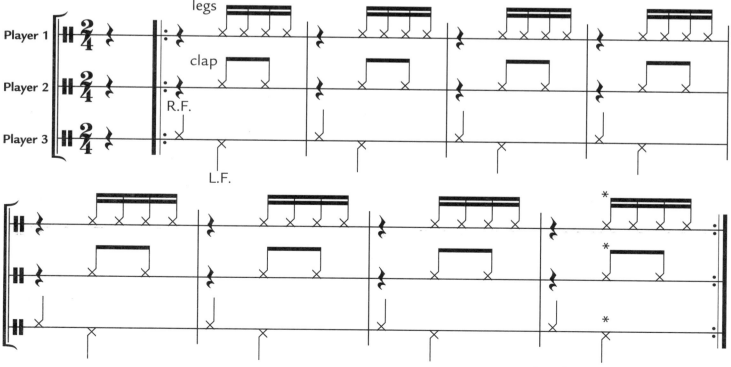

21

*Play first seven times only.

Introducing the Dotted Eighth and Sixteenth Note:

A dot (•) placed after a note increases the note's length by one-half the original value.

Example:

Practice Warm-Up

Practice the following rhythm patterns until you are comfortable with them.
Start slowly, and gradually increase the tempo. Be sure to count!

1.

Count: 1 e & a 2   3 e & a 4

2.

Count: 1 e & a 2 e & a 3   4

3.

Count: 1 e & a 2 & 3 e & a 4 &

4.

Count: 1 e & a 2 e & a 3 & 4 &

5.

Count: 1   2 e & a 3   4 e & a

6.

Count: 1 e & a 2 e & a 3 e & a 4 e & a

If You're Happy and You Know It

 Track 17

Before playing along with the CD, practice the part alone until you are comfortable with it. Start slowly and gradually increase the tempo.

Moderato (♩ = 112)

Count: 1 2 3 4 e & a

mf If you're hap - py and you know it, clap your hands. (clap clap) If you're

hap - py and you know it, clap your hands. (clap clap) If you're hap - py and you know it, then you

real - ly ought to show it, If you're hap - py and you know it, clap your hands. (clap clap)

* Play first time only.

22

Sho-Jo-Ji  Track 18
(A Japanese Folk Song)

Before playing along with the CD, practice the part alone until you are comfortable with it. Start slowly and increase the tempo.

Dotted Eighth and Sixteenth-Note Duet Track 19

Use two different sound sources for this duet. Before playing along with the CD, practice each part separately until you are comfortable with it. Start slowly and gradually increase the tempo.

El Rabel  Track 20
(A Chilean Folk Song)

Use three different sound sources for this song.
Before playing along with the CD, practice each
part separately until you are comfortable with it.
Start slowly and gradually increase the tempo.

Play nine times.

Body Drumming

Use three different sound sources (hands, legs, chest, etc.).

Play nine times.

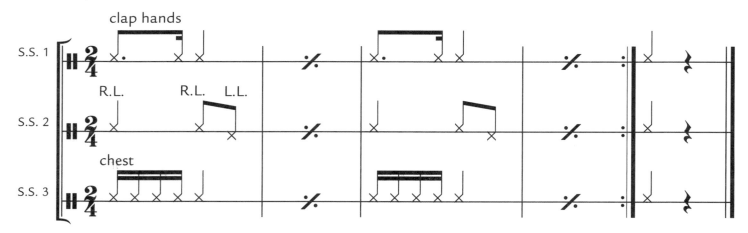

Review: $\frac{6}{8}$ Time

6 means there are six beats in each measure.
8 means an eighth note (♪) gets one beat.

For the following rhythms, clap or tap
once for each note, counting aloud.

Dotted quarter note (♩.)
or rests (𝄽 ♩) = 3 beats
(Count: 1 2 3)

Quarter note (♩)
or quarter rest (𝄽) = 2 beats
(Count: 1 2)

Eighth note (♪)
or eighth rest (♪) = 1 beat
(Count: 1)

$\frac{6}{8}$ Duet Track 21

Use two different sound sources for this duet. Before playing along with
the CD, practice each part separately until you are comfortable with it.
Start slowly and gradually increase the tempo.

Tarantella Track 22
(An Italian Dance)

Before playing along with the CD, practice each part separately until you are comfortable with it. You may play the top line on either a sound source, or by patting the top of your leg. Start slowly and gradually increase the the tempo.

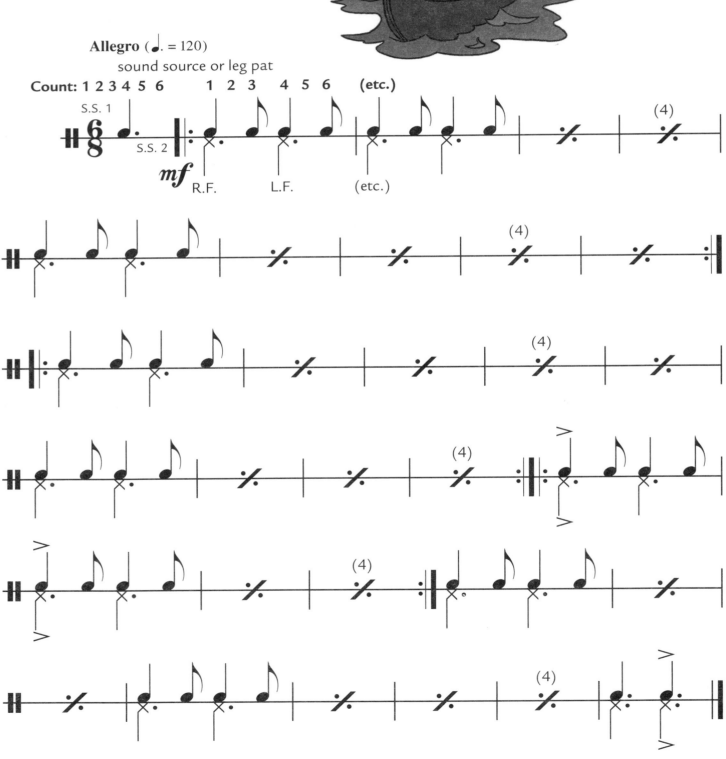

Review: Improvisation

A slash with or without a stem (♪ or /) equals one beat in $\frac{6}{8}$ time. This symbol means to improvise (compose on the spur of the moment) by choosing any of the sound sources you've used so far.

Practice Warm-Up Track 23

Before playing along with the CD, practice the following part alone until you are comfortable with it. Start slowly, and gradually increase the tempo. When you get to the part where you improvise, use some of the rhythms you've already learned.

Play the first line seven times.

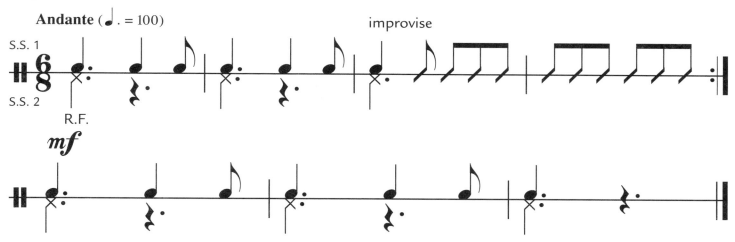

Body Drumming

Use two different sound sources (hands, feet, etc.).
Both parts can be played by one person.

Play the first line seven times.

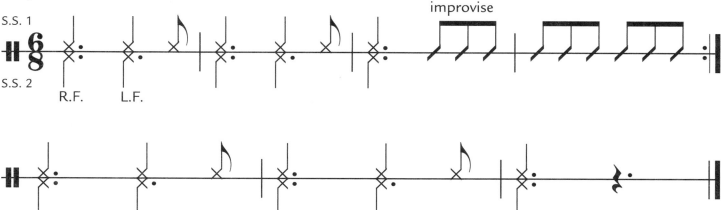

Introducing Four New Rhythms

Practice the following rhythm patterns until you are comfortable with them. Listen to the first measure of each exercise, and then echo (play) the same rhythm pattern in the second measure. Start slowly, and gradually increase the tempo. Be sure to count.

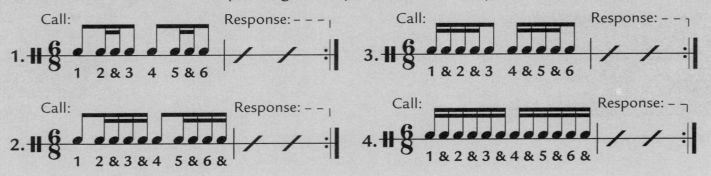

Arroz con Leche Track 25

(A Puerto Rican Folk Song)

Before playing along with the CD, practice the part alone until you are comfortable with it. Start slowly and gradually increase the tempo. When improvising, you may use any of the new rhythms above.

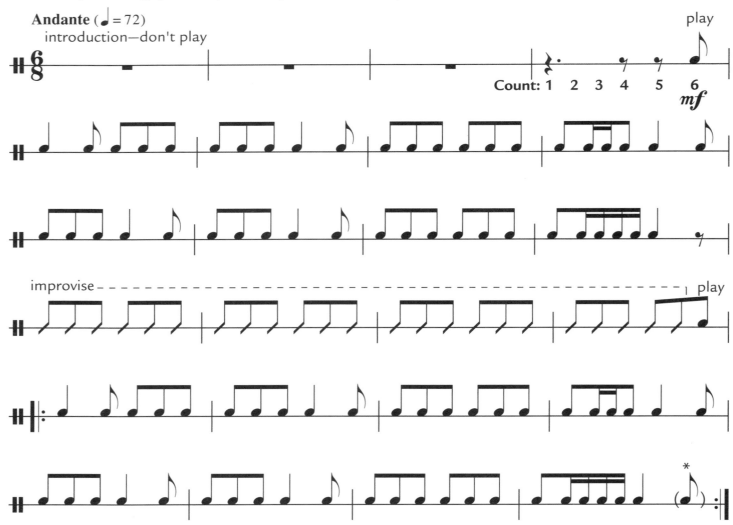

*Play first time only.

The Kerry Dance
 Track 26
(An Irish Dance)

Use two different sound sources for this song.
Before playing along with the CD, practice each
part separately until you are comfortable with it.

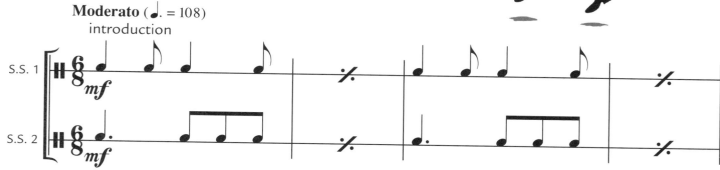

Play four times.

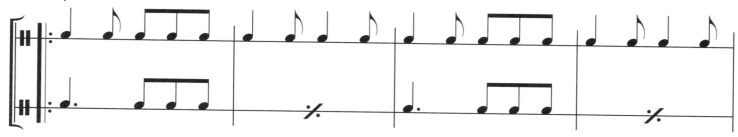

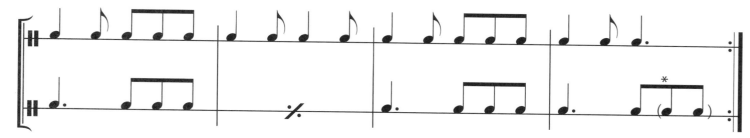

*Play first three times only.

Body Drumming

Use two different sound sources (hands, feet, etc.). Both parts can be played by one person.

Play nine times.

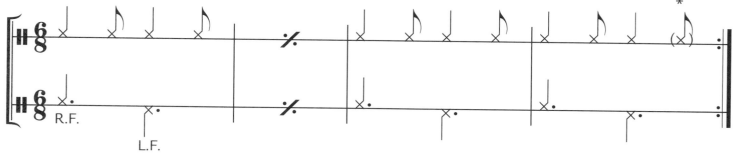

*Play first eight times only.

Review: Syncopation

Notes that are played between the main beats of a measure and held across the beat are called *syncopated* notes. In the first rhythm, the first quarter note is syncopated because it is played on "&" and held across beat 2.

Syncopation also occurs when a note that is one beat or longer starts on an "&". In the third example, the first note is syncopated because it is one beat long and starts on "&".

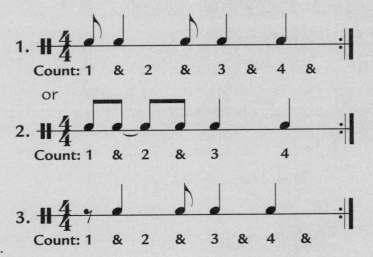

Practice Warm-Up  Track 27

Practice the following rhythm patterns separately until you are comfortable with them. Start slowly, and gradually increase the tempo. Remember to count carefully and keep a steady pulse!

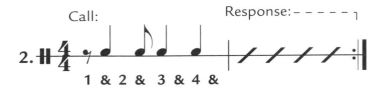

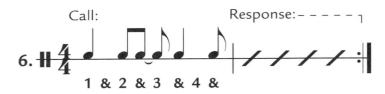

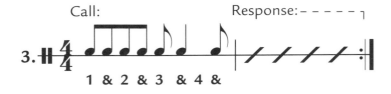

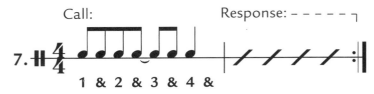

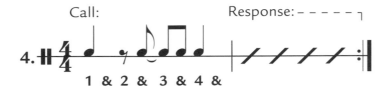

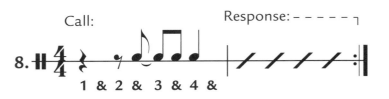

Syncopation Duet Track 28

Use two different sound sources for this duet. Before playing along with the CD, practice each part separately until you are comfortable with it. Start slowly and gradually increase the tempo.

Nobody's Business Track 29

(A Jamaican Folk Song)

This song is in a style of music called *calypso*. Use three different sound sources for this song. Before playing along with the CD, practice each part separately until you are comfortable with it. Start slowly and gradually increase the tempo.

Play four times.

31

*Play first three times only.

Body Drumming—Nobody's Business Track 29

Use three different sound sources (hands, feet, chest, etc.).

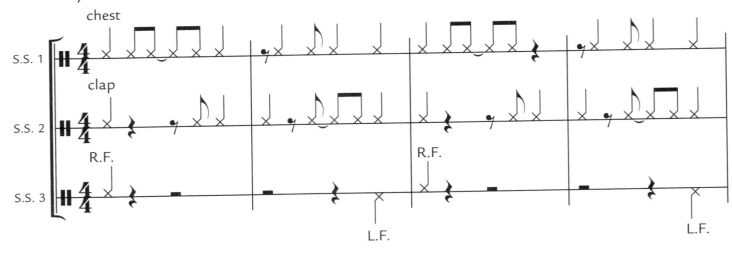

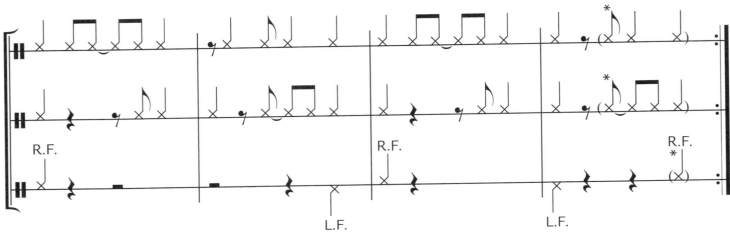

*Play first three times only.

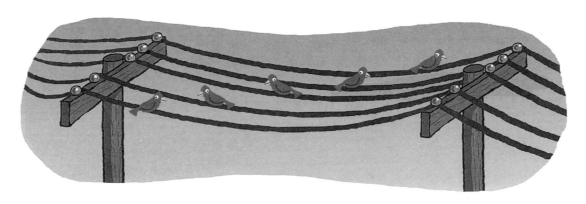

Review: Five-Line Staff

A standard staff is
made up of five lines
and the four spaces
between those lines.

Introducing Drumset Notation

Up until this point, the notes for the drums/sound sources have been written on a staff with either one, two or three lines.

When using five lines, each line and space of the staff is assigned to a particular drum, cymbal or sound source.

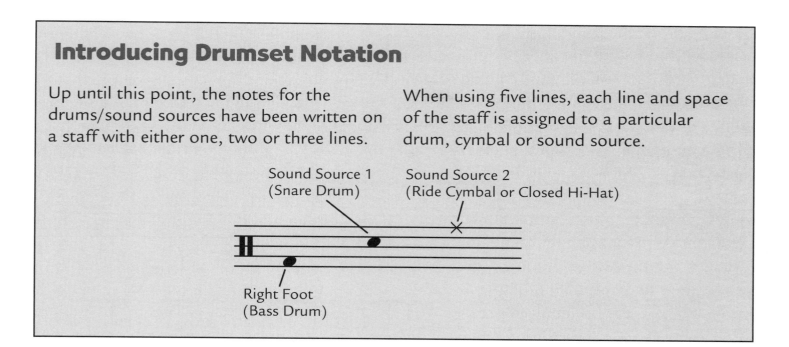

Sound Source 1 (Snare Drum)

Sound Source 2 (Ride Cymbal or Closed Hi-Hat)

Right Foot (Bass Drum)

Practice Warm-Up Track 30

In the following exercise, we are going to play an imaginary drumset using a combination of sound sources and body drumming. Practice the exercise alone until you are comfortable with it. Be sure to count!

right hand on sound source or right knee

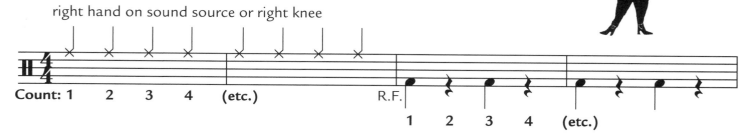

Count: 1   2   3   4   (etc.)   R.F.   1   2   3   4   (etc.)

left hand on sound source or left knee

Twinkle, Twinkle, Little Star Track 31

Before playing along with the CD, practice the part alone until you are comfortable with it. Start slowly and gradually increase the tempo.
Play three times.

Andante (♩ = 88)

mf

*Play first two times only.

Practice Warm-Up Track 32

In the following exercise, we are going to play an imaginary drumset using a combination of sound sources and body drumming. Practice the exercise alone until you are comfortable with it. Be sure to count!

right hand on sound source or right knee

Count: 1 & 2 & 3 & 4 & (etc.)

R.F.

1 2 & 3 4 (etc.)

left hand on sound source or left knee

Old MacDonald Had a Farm  Track 33

Before playing along with the CD, practice the part alone until you are comfortable with it. Start slowly and gradually increase the tempo.

Play two times.

Andante (♩ = 80)

mf

*Play first time only.

Ahg-Doom Bahg-Doom

Track 34

(An Indian Folk Song)

Before playing along with the CD, practice the part alone until you are comfortable with it. Start slowly and gradually increase the tempo.

Andante (♩ = 76)

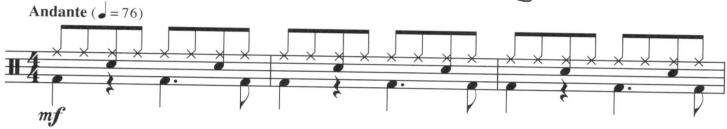

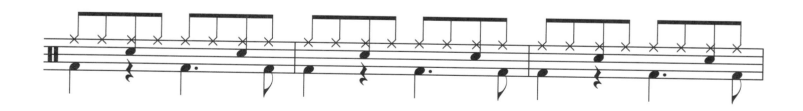

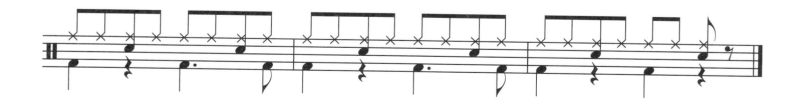

Introducing The Two-Beat Rhythm

The *two-beat rhythm* is common in Broadway show tunes, circus music, country music and folk tunes.

Russian Dance Track 35

Before playing along with the CD, practice the part alone until you are comfortable with it. Start slowly and gradually increase the tempo.

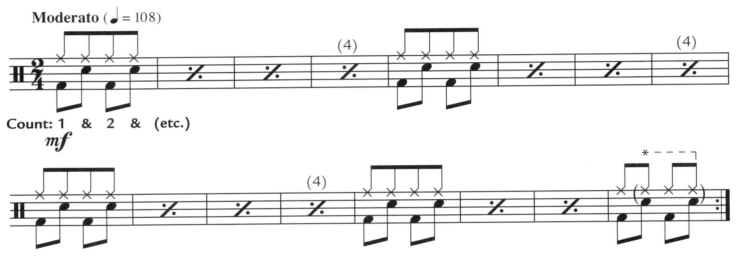

Moderato (♩ = 108)

Count: 1 & 2 & (etc.)

mf

*Play first time only.

Body Drumming

Use two different sound sources (hands, feet, etc.).

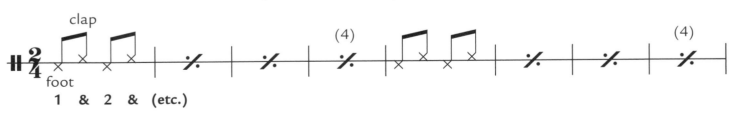

clap

foot

1 & 2 & (etc.)

*Play first time only.

Turkey In The Straw  Track 36

Before playing along with the CD, practice the part alone until you are comfortable with it. Start slowly and gradually increase the tempo.

Andante ($\quad$ = 88)

Count: 1 2   1 & 2 & (etc.)

*Play first time only.

Body Drumming

Use two different sound sources (hands, feet, etc.).

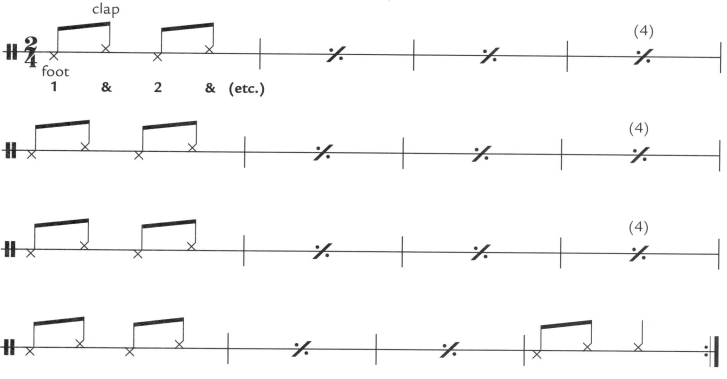

1 & 2 & (etc.)

Siyahamba  Track 37
(A South African Zulu Song)

Before playing along with the CD, practice
the part alone until you are comfortable with it.
Start slowly and gradually increase the tempo.

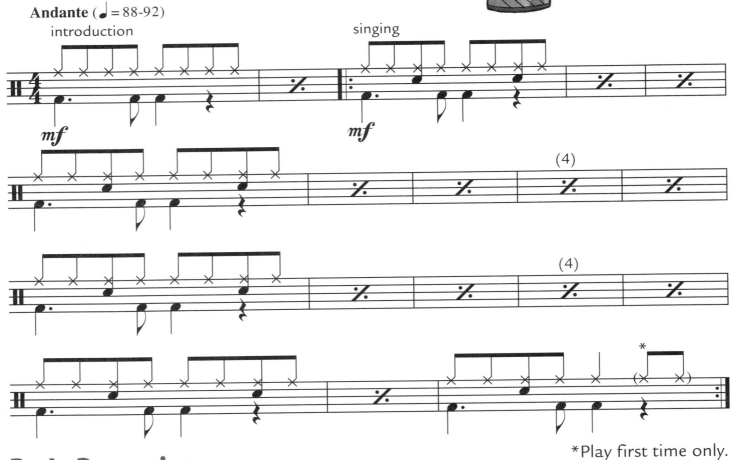

*Play first time only.

Body Drumming

Use two different sound sources (hands, feet, etc.).

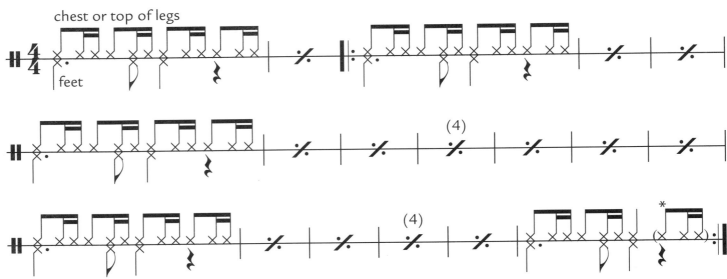

*Play first time only.

Certificate of Completion

This certifies that

_____

has mastered and perfected

Book 2 of Alfred's Kid's Drum Course

_____
Teacher / Parent

_____
Date

Recording Credits

Ahg-Doom Bahg-Doom
This recording is from *Games Children Sing-India*, by Gloria J. Kiester,
Ⓟ© 2005 Alfred Publishing Co., Inc. Used with Permission.

Sha Lee Hung Ba
This recording is from *Games Children Sing-China*, by Gloria J. Kiester,
Ⓟ© 2005 Alfred Publishing Co., Inc. Used with Permission.

Grasshopper
This recording is from *Games Children Sing-Japan*, by Gloria J. Kiester/Mika Kimula,
Ⓟ© 2005 Alfred Publishing Co., Inc. Used with Permission.

Hi-Yah-Ho
This recording is from *Games Children Sing-China*, by Gloria J. Kiester,
Ⓟ© 2005 Alfred Publishing Co., Inc. Used with Permission.

Sho-Jo-Ji
This recording is from *Games Children Sing-Japan*, by Gloria J. Kiester/Mika Kimula,
Ⓟ© 2005 Alfred Publishing Co., Inc. Used with Permission.

Chacarera
This recording is from *Songs of Latin America*, by Patricia Shehan Campbell and
Ana Lucia Frega, Ⓟ© 2001 Alfred Publishing Co., Inc. Used with Permission.

Cajueiro Pequenino
This recording is from *Songs of Latin America*, by Patricia Shehan Campbell and
Ana Lucia Frega, Ⓟ© 2001 Alfred Publishing Co., Inc. Used with Permission.

El Rabel
This recording is from *Songs of Latin America*, by Patricia Shehan Campbell and
Ana Lucia Frega, Ⓟ© 2001 Alfred Publishing Co., Inc. Used with Permission.

Arroz con Leche
This recording is from *Songs of Latin America*, by Patricia Shehan Campbell and
Ana Lucia Frega, Ⓟ© 2001 Alfred Publishing Co., Inc. Used with Permission.

La Bamba
This recording is from *Mexican Folk Dances*, edited by Debbie Cavalier,
Ⓟ© 2001 Alfred Publishing, Inc. Used with Permission.

Paru-Paraong Bukid
This recording is from *Games Children Sing Around the World*, edited by Paul Ramsier,
Ⓟ© 1994 Alfred Publishing Co., Inc. Used with Permission.

Don Simone
This recording is from *Songs of Hispanic Americans*, by Ruth De Cesare,
Ⓟ© 1991 Alfred Publishing Co., Inc. Used with Permission.

Siyahamba
This recording is from *A Small Part of the World*, by Sally K. Albrecht,
Ⓟ© 1997 Alfred Publishing Co., Inc. Used with permission.